To my beloved Velma & Osmin

TELL ME WHO'S WONDERFUL

By
Jo Clem

Jo Clem

Illustrations by Mary Cooley Craddock

Tell Me Who's Wonderful
by Jo Clem

Printed in the United States of America

ISBN 9781628712605

Illustrated by Mary Cooley Craddock

www.xulonpress.com

This book is dedicated to my three precious children, Jamie, Kevin and Kelly, who taught me what it means to be wonderful. They **all** know **the** answer to the question. It is, "*Me ... I am wonderful.*"

Foreword

This book is the *banner* of my life ... a message and a legacy I want to leave behind. It is a simple story regarding a simple question we all need to ask and answer. Readers need not take my word for this; the Father Himself, in Psalms 139, tells us of the *wonder* of who we are: "I knit you together in your mother's womb. You are fearfully and wonderfully made."

In my early twenties, my dad was suddenly called home to be with the Lord. I had spoken with him the night before, and all seemed fine. When I got the news of his passing, I wondered if he knew how much I loved him and how wonderful he was. If only I had had one more chance to tell him. I decided I would never again be in this place. I would make sure those I love know of my love and just how wonderful they are.

Blessed with children of my own, I made sure they were able to answer the question from the time they learned to speak.

I see the results of this consistent encouragement and support in their lives and in the lives of my grandchildren.

My prayer is that all who read this tender story will also choose to give the gift of love and certainty to their relationships.

It only takes a moment each day to verbalize the love we have for others. We never know the difference that reassurance will make in their lives, that day and for always.

From the window seat, Abigail watched the
big flakes of snow settle on the sidewalk.

She loved watching the snow and hearing
the fire crackle in the living room nearby.

It won't be long now, she thought. The hands on the grandfather clock were almost there ... straight up and straight down ... six o'clock, a very special time of day.

Daddy would soon be coming up the sidewalk, and their special time together would begin.

Abigail had already placed her father's slippers beside his chair.

Abigail's Mommy was feeding her little brother, David, in the kitchen. Smells of supper filled the air.

"I wonder what's for dinner?" Abigail thought. She'd like to go ask her Mommy, but she did not want to miss her Daddy's arrival. She settled into her cozy, watchful spot by the window.

The tires of the bus made a crunching sound in the snow on
the street. Daddy stepped out, already waving to Abigail in
her familiar perch at the window.

Smiling as he neared the house, she giggled at the thought of how he would come in, stomp the snow off his shoes and say, "Burrrrrrr!"

Then he would lean down to hug her, even before he took off his coat.

Together, they would go back to greet Mommy and Baby David.

Then it would be time for her to answer "the questions," and she knew just how that would go.

Rocker, slippers, then up she'd crawl, and Daddy would say, "So, Abigail, tell me about your day."

Abigail told Daddy about school and friends and seeing neighbors building a snowman.

They'd rock a bit and silently sit ... knowing
the most fun was yet to come.

"Now Abigail," Daddy smiled as he gave her a hug.

"I have a question for you."

Abigail was smiling too and could hardly wait to play their game.

"So ... tell me ... who's wonderful?"

Every day it was the same. She
would think of all the people
who were wonderful and
name them off. "Mommy is
wonderful … "

"Yes," said Daddy, "and who else?"
"Baby David … "

"Yes," Daddy smiled, "and who else?"

"Grammy is wonderful ... "

"For sure," said Daddy, "and who else?"

"Nana and Papa ... and all my cousins." Giggling with excitement, as she knew their game was going well, Abigail said, "And you, Daddy ... you are wonderful, too!"

Once, a while ago, Abigail asked Daddy how he first knew that he was wonderful.

Daddy smiled and said, "Oh ... that's an easy question. Your Grammy told me so."

In fact, he told her that when he was a little boy, he played this very same game with his Mom, Dad, and his two sisters.

Abigail smiled as she thought of them; they were wonderful too.

Grammy said the psalmist David tells us so ...

"For you, Father, created me; you knit me together
in my mother's womb. I praise you because I am
fearfully and wonderfully made."
Psalms 139

Abigail knew that even though David was just a baby, someday he would learn to answer the question, too. She was his big sister, and she planned to help him learn the answer.

Now it was time for Daddy to put David to bed. Abigail went in to have dinner with Mommy and Daddy.

She loved this time to just be with them ... like it was
before she had a baby brother.

After dinner, Daddy helped with the dishes and she and
Mommy read books together.

Soon it was her bedtime, too.

Mommy helped as Abigail had her bath, brushed her teeth
and slipped into her pajamas.

Then Mommy and Daddy listened as she said her prayers
and they would ask her one more time ...

"Abigail ... who is wonderful?"
Abigail loved keeping the one answer she knew
they wanted to hear until this last, cozy moment.

"Me," she said. "I AM WONDERFUL."

"That's right little one; YOU are wonderful."

CPSIA information can be obtained at www.ICGtesting.com
Printed in the USA
LVIW01n0412230515
439496LV00001B/2